Who Are You?

Who Are You?

*Finding Your Identity in
Being a Child of God*

Stacy Miller, MA LPCC

WESTBOW
P R E S S®
A DIVISION OF THOMAS NELSON
& ZONDERVAN

WestBow Press books may be ordered through booksellers or by contacting:

WestBow Press
A Division of Thomas Nelson & Zondervan
1663 Liberty Drive
Bloomington, IN 47403
www.westbowpress.com
1 (866) 928-1240

ISBN: 978-1-4908-9502-4 (sc)
ISBN: 978-1-4908-9504-8 (hc)
ISBN: 978-1-4908-9503-1 (e)

Print information available on the last page.

WestBow Press rev. date: 09/08/2015

To God, my Father, Abba~
Thank You for guiding me through this continual journey of finding my identity in being completely Yours.

To my husband, thank you for being so supportive and encouraging this dream. I love you.

Thank you to everyone- family, friends, and others who supported and encouraged this dream and the message behind this book.

*For the eyes of the Lord move to and fro
throughout the Earth, that He may strongly
support those whose heart is completely His..
2 Chronicles 16:9 (NASB)*

TABLE OF CONTENTS

INTRODUCTION ~ The Journey Begins

Before I begin this book, I feel led to share my heart with you. Everything I write about in this book is based on *experiences*. It is based on my own personal experiences and experiences I've observed others going through and have gone through. I believe that everyone at some point in their life faces a time where they are "finding themselves." I've personally found my identity in the past in a variety of different things including relationships, family, ministry, athletics, and seeking approval from others. So know as you are reading, that I've been there and I'm still learning. I believe that finding you're identity in God is a lifelong journey and process. If you are in a place of searching, God wants to answer your questions. If you are in a place of brokenness, God wants to heal your heart. If you are in a place of feeling lost, God desires to help you find your way. If you are in a place of finding yourself and who you are, God wants to give you an identity that comes with promises and hope beyond your wildest dreams.

Listening for God

We walk into our worship services and pray "Holy Spirit come," or "we invite your presence here with us" or "Lord, we just want to hear you speak!" But do we really? Think about the amount of time a typical church spends doing, serving, planning, studying, reading, organizing, talking, programming, etc. What % of our time doing Christian "stuff" involves listening? Write below an estimate of what percent of our time as Christians is spent listening for God in your opinion:

_____%

If the percentage you wrote down was low, why do you think that is? Why would we want to avoid listening for a perfect God to show us something in our lives?

It seems that often the thing that keeps us from listening is fear of what God may reveal to us when we listen.

The reason I share this concept in the introduction of this book is because the format of the book is set for the reader to spend a lot of time reading *and* listening for what God would individually want to show them in their lives. *I truly believe that a small part of what you will receive from this book is the content, and a large part of what you will receive is what God shows you individually in your time spent with Him in reflection of the content.*

Take as much time as you need to process what God is showing you personally. I encourage you to slowly make your way through this book. Some of the interactive activities and reflection questions may require some processing time.

This is written in a format where it may be used as a book and/or workbook. There are opportunities throughout the book for drawing and writing. There are also reflection questions at the end of each chapter for small group settings or for individual use. You can either use the book itself to record your thoughts or you may want to use a separate journal.

My prayer is that if you are struggling with finding out who you are, no matter what stage in your journey, that this book will take you at least one step closer to a deeper understanding that *you are a child of God*. Also, that the promises and security that come with being a child of the King are worth putting your identity in.

I hope that you will take this journey and that it will leave you changed.

So this is where the journey begins...

CHAPTER 1 ~ Who Are You?

*"How great is the love the Father has lavished on us, that **we should be called children of God**! And that is what we are!"*
~1 John 3:1(NIV)

You may have seen the movie *Eat Pray Love*. When I began the journey of "finding myself" in God, this movie was an avenue that God used to teach me. It is a movie about a woman, played by Julia Roberts, who comes to a place in her life where she is finding out who she is. Her whole life she has had a dream of traveling so she decides to travel across the world for a year to find out who she is. The first place she goes is Italy. In one of these scenes, she is at a restaurant with her new friends. They are getting to know her. Someone sitting next to her asks her what word would describe who she is. She thinks about the question for a while and responds with "writer." After all, that is what she was doing for her career. A man sitting next to her responds:

"That's what you *do*. That's not **who you are**."

So the woman continues on through the movie to find the answer to the question of who she is apart from what she does.

As I watched this scene in the movie, my eyes were filled with tears. I began to ask myself the question "**Who am I** apart from what I do?" "**Who am I** apart from the areas I try to perform in?" I had a very hard time identifying anything. I believe a lot of us define ourselves in what we do rather than in who we are. I began to process this question, and a phrase continued to come to my mind over and over and over again....

A child of God...

I am a child of God.

That is who I am.

As the concept began to sink in, my mind began traveling a mile a minute to determine what that really means. What does it *really* mean to be a child of God? What does it mean to have our **full security** and **foundation** in being a child of God?

It seems that society teaches us to put our identity in everything but him. When we watch commercials on TV, we find ourselves wanting the next big purchase that will make us happy and when we finally get it, it always falls short of what we're really searching for deep down. When we watch movies and TV shows we see identities in people's professions, hobbies, financial status, body image, spouses, and children. Again, they all seem to fall short of the peace our heart desires.

Even within our churches today, we find ourselves putting identities in church "stuff" instead of God. We see identities being found in people's ministries instead of the God that desires to be glorified in their ministry. We see identities being found in the individual church itself, church programs, and in other people within the church. However, when we stop, slow down, and really listen to

> You are a child of God. That is who you are.

what our heart's desire is, we find that none of these things or people are enough to fill that deep desire that we are longing to fulfill.

There is a difference between *having a relationship with God* and having your *identity in God*. To have your identity in someone means they define who you are and your self-worth. Your sense of security is found in that person. There is more to risk in finding your identity in God than in just having a relationship with him. However, there is also more to gain. We will discuss this concept more in later chapters.

Do you know who you are? Do you put your identity in someone or something other than God? Maybe you want your identity to be in being a child of God, but you don't know how or where to start. As we begin this journey, imagine someone you just met asking you to describe who you are in a few words. What would you *honestly* say? Write it below:

I believe that the Lord wants more than anything else for our hearts to be fully his. I encourage you as we close this first chapter to really open up your ears, heart, and mind to what he may want to reveal to you. There may be something very near to your heart that he wants to show you, even right now. Listen and experience all he has for you as his child.

Chapter 1 Reflection Questions

1. If you were to describe what your identity is in today honestly, how would you describe it?

2. What have you observed society and the media teaching you to put your identity in?

3. In what way do you think having your identity in God would affect your daily life?

CHAPTER 2 ~ The Child in the Crowd

At that time the disciples came to Jesus, saying "Who is the greatest in the kingdom of heaven?" And calling to him a child, he put him in the midst of them and said, "Truly, I say to you, unless you turn and become like children, you will never enter the kingdom of heaven. Whoever humbles himself like this child is the greatest in the kingdom of heaven."

Whoever receives one such child in my name receives me, but whoever causes one of these little ones who believe in me to sin, it would be better for him to have a great millstone fastened around his neck and to be drowned in the depth of the sea."
~Matthew 18:1-6 (ESV)

Read those verses again slowly and visualize being physically there when the disciples go to Jesus.

First, you have the disciples coming to Jesus basically asking "Who is the best?" Jesus immediately finds a child from the crowd, calls the child over to him, and has the child stand right in the middle of the disciples (I wonder if he was sending a message even in having the child stand "in the midst" of the disciples?).

How often do we see *striving* in our churches? I'm not talking about striving to become more like Jesus, I'm talking about striving to impress the person sitting next to us in a pew. I'm talking about striving to be the most spiritual, to serve the most, to bring the most people in, to be the best. As I am writing, the word "trap" comes to mind. Striving is a trap because it's never enough. Once you start striving, it leaves you feeling empty so you keep striving more and more, looking for contentment that you never receive. There is nothing wrong with serving and looking to follow God with your actions, but it seems that if those things become the **foundation** of your faith, it is never enough. It sounds like the disciples were *striving* in Matthew 18. They were looking to find who was the greatest.

Become Like This Child

Jesus calls out the disciples and tells them to change and become like the child in front of them. Then he answers their original question and says that those who humble themselves like the child are the greatest. He emphasizes being *humble*.

In the New Testament, Jesus often teaches by signs, representations, and parables. Jesus calling that child from the crowd was *representing* something in his teaching. There is something about the life, innocence, humility and being of a child that represents what God desires for us.

"Unless you **turn** and become like children, you will never enter the kingdom of heaven." Think about how Jesus said to "turn" and become like children. If you are facing one direction and heading in that direction and you *turn*, then you will be heading in a completely different direction than before. You will also end up at a completely different destination. Therefore, Jesus is saying that unless they become like children, they will not be headed in the right direction. It sounds like it is crucial to turn.

Jesus says that whoever receives a child in his name will likewise receive him. He compares causing a child to sin with having a great millstone fastened around your neck and being drowned in the depths of the sea. Wow. Jesus is *very* protective of little children and even calls their humility *the greatest in the kingdom of heaven.*

I wonder what the disciples were feeling at this point. Foolish? Humbled? Maybe they were feeling a little confused. Maybe they were thinking something like "Jesus wants us to be like a little child. Here I have been spending all this time trying to out-spiritualize the disciple next to me and impress Jesus and others so I can be the greatest, yet he says that the greatest will be a little innocent child?"

Let's go back to the concept of finding ourselves in who we are, not what we do. The disciples asked, "Who is the greatest in the Kingdom of Heaven?" I'm wondering if that question was another way of asking what we have to *do* to be the best.

Jesus responded with, *be. Be* like this little child. Children don't feel the need to perform or impress because they are innocent. Whatever they think, they say. Whatever they feel, they do. There is not pride or performance involved. They just *are.* They experience freedom in just *being.* Is there any area in your life where you find yourself trying to perform for God or others instead of "being?"

> Children experience freedom by simply **being**

What does it mean to *be* as a child of God? When I hear the word "be," I think of *contentment, natural, and peace.* When I think of "being the best" as asked by the disciples, I think of *pressure, competition, pride, and forced.*

Is our **identity** in *being a child of God* or in trying to be the best? *Being* will look different for each individual based on how God uniquely created them. We will discuss this more in the *Uniquely You* chapter.

7

> *"O Father, Lord of heaven and earth, thank you for*
> *hiding these things from those who think themselves*
> *wise and clever, and for revealing them to the childlike.*
> *Yes, Father, it pleased you to do it this way!"*
> *~Matthew 11:25-26 (NLT)*

In this verse, Jesus is making a direct comparison between "those who think themselves wise and clever" and those who are "childlike." It's interesting that in the majority of Scriptures where Jesus discusses children, he is teaching on pride in some way. God *blesses the humble* with wisdom and withholds wisdom from the proud. Why do you think that is?

As we continue this journey, we will take a look at additional Scriptures where God discusses children. We will also take a look at the lives and attributes of children and the freedom that God desires for us as his children.

****

Let's close with this illustration, where you, the reader, will be the child in the crowd in Matthew 18:1-6. This illustration is based on what the child in the crowd may have been feeling throughout the passage. It may be helpful to read this slowly and out loud if you are alone:

Watching. It's so awesome to watch this "Jesus" person. I want to be as close to him as possible but I don't know why. He's different than most adults I know. Sometimes I feel worried when I'm around adults, but when I look at him, I feel calm. I wonder if he notices me? Even if he doesn't- it's okay, I just want to be close to him.

I see these adults called "disciples" asking him something. They are standing right next to him. I think they asked him something like, who is the best in the Kingdom of Heaven? I don't know why they are asking something like that, they are so lucky to just be able to be with him all the time. They just don't get it.

Everytime I look at Jesus, I get goosebumps all over me, and I can't stop smiling. I want to cry, but not a sad cry. I've heard this word before that adults use, I think that word is what I am feeling right now. The word is "peace."

Wait! Jesus just looked at me, called me, and asked me to come stand with him and the disciples! The closer I get to him, the more I start to cry. More than ever, I want to sit on his lap, to hug him, just to look at him. He has me stand in the middle of all of the disciples and told the disciples to change and become like me?

Why me? I'm not as smart as the disciples. I don't know how to use all the fancy words like they use. I'm just a child who wants to be with Jesus.

Standing so close to him, I feel so protected. He reminds me of the gentleness of a lamb and the strength of a lion. The closer I get to him, the more I feel like I can trust him. Like I can trust him more than any person I know. I feel like he will never leave my side even if I can't see him standing next to me. He just looked at me. His eyes are like nothing I've ever seen before. He looked me right in the eyes and just stared at me and smiled at me. As he stares at me, I feel like I want to sleep because of how calm I feel.

*I want this Jesus to be my best friend. I want him to be my papa, my daddy. I want him to be the new King. More than anything, I just want to **be** with him…*

Chapter 2 Reflection Questions

1. What did you feel emotionally when you put yourself in the shoes of the child in the crowd in the last story?

2. Do you feel those same emotions when you interact with God on a daily basis or do you feel something different? If different, why do you think that is?

3. Do you feel like you can relate more to the disciples or to the child in Matthew 18:1-6?

4. Do you find yourself "performing" for God or others or simply "being?" If you find yourself performing for God or others, why is that?

CHAPTER 3 ~ Freedom...In All Things

The soul is healed by being with children.
~English Proverb

One thing I adore about children is their innocence and inability to care what people think of them. They experience **freedom**. They are free to be themselves.

One day my husband and I went into a video game and music store, and there was a little boy there who looked around the age of 7 or 8. He was being very loud and vocal due to excitement about the games he was going to be getting. He looked up at his mom and said, "Mommy, I love video games so much. I am a video game expert. I know *everything* about video games!!" I laughed inside when I heard this and got a huge smile on my face. This boy didn't care how anyone else around the store was observing him. He was just himself. He said what was on his mind and heart. If an adult was doing the exact thing that child was- other adults probably would have thought things like the following. "He needs to quiet down." "Who does he think he is?" "Does he think he knows everything?"

Does God desire for us to have innocence like this child? If so, in what ways? Should the church be a place that cherishes and encourages this seeking of innocence?

So often we hear teaching after teaching that emphasizes "spiritual disciplines" daily. This includes emphasis on prayer, reading the Bible, etc. every day. And there is nothing wrong with this emphasis. Emphasis on these disciplines is not only important it is vital. But are we missing an emphasis on other avenues in addition?

Are these "spiritual disciplines" the *only* way to experience God? Are you experiencing God if you go outside and sit in his creation? Are you experiencing God by experiencing love within your family? If you're not a reader, can you experience God just as much through singing? What about through painting? What about when you are spending time with a child?

The questions I'm posing are the following. Can experiencing God be a constant, natural lifestyle instead of one increment of reading and prayer during the day? What if all these things are ways to experience God even if you don't say the word "God" when doing them?

I feel the need to clarify here that finding other avenues to experience God are not to *replace* exposing ourselves to God's Word consistently; they are *in addition* to God's Word. However, exposing ourselves to God's Word consistently may look different for each individual. Exposing ourselves to His Word may mean taking one specific verse and meditating on it all week long. Exposing ourselves to His Word may mean going through an in-depth group Bible study. It may mean sitting down alone and working through a chapter. It may mean listening to a teaching. It may vary depending on the season you are going through in your life. It may mean 10 minutes a day or 2 hours a day. There is no formula involved.

In the next chapter we will talk about *balance*. It's important to find a balance between spiritual disciplines and experiencing God in all things. What balance looks like in your life individually may look different than the person next to you. However, if you allow God to show you that balance, it will bring *freedom.*

The Word Gave Life to Everything

In the beginning the Word already existed. The Word was with God, and the Word was God. He existed in the beginning with God. God created everything through Him, and nothing was created except through Him. **The Word gave life to everything that was created, and His life brought light to everyone.** *The light shines in the darkness, and the darkness can never extinguish it. God sent a man, John the Baptist, to tell about the light so that everyone might believe because of his testimony. John himself was not the light; he was simply a witness to tell about the light. The One who is the true light, who gives light to everyone was coming into the world.*
~John 1:1-9 (NLT)

We start verse one with "in the beginning." Sound familiar? The very first verse in Genesis also begins with "in the beginning." So it appears that John is introducing a foundational concept.

God created *everything* and then *gave life* to that creation (vs. 3-4). Notice, it doesn't say any of the following in those verses:

God *only* created the Bible.

God *only* created prayer.

God *only* created Sunday morning church.

God *only* created spiritual conversations.

No, it says he created *everything* through Jesus. Like a child with a vivid imagination and innocence, can *everything* be an opportunity to experience God? It's interesting that God told us to turn and become like a child, because children can barely read, more the less understand the depth of Scripture. Children *experience* God in everything good and pure. There is a sense of awe in their perspective on life.

I feel the need to add here that "everything" described above does not include sin. God cannot bless sin. He is not the creator of sin. When I say "everything," I mean everything that he is the creator of. Notice in John 1:4, "the Word gave life to everything *that was created.*" This includes his creation, his people, and the things that his people have created that are good and pure.

> *God sent a man, John the Baptist, to tell about the light*
> *so that everyone might believe because of his testimony.*
> *John himself was not the light; he was simply a witness to*
> *tell about the light. The One who is the true light, who*
> *gives light to everyone was coming into the world.*
> *~John 1:9 (NLT)*

John the Baptist is brought into the picture, a man who was described as a witness to tell about the light. John the Baptist was an avenue to help people experience God. The Bible is an avenue to help people experience God. But what if there are more avenues than just the Bible and people talking about God? What if *everything* can be used as an avenue to experience God?

God created us so uniquely. He created us with specific gifts, personalities, love languages, and he has us experience all kinds of different life circumstances. Someone who uses the gift of intercession is just as glorifying to God as someone who uses the gift of teaching. Someone who expresses love through the language of words of affirmation is just as glorifying to God as someone who expresses love through the language of gifts. Someone who is extroverted is just as glorifying as someone who is introverted. Someone who is in a "secular" career field is just as glorifying to God as someone who is in full-time ministry. God created *everything* and his *light* brought *life* to *everything*.

When I counsel, we have a specific set of questions that take place during the first few sessions of seeing people. One of the questions asked is: What are your interests? What do you enjoy doing? I see children, teenagers, and adults and it never seizes to amaze me how easily a child can answer this question. Adults tend to struggle more with it. A child would quickly answer something like "I love drawing, playing outside, playing video games, playing with my dog, reading, etc." Adults may struggle more, and it may take them awhile to even think of one thing. It seems that as we get older, we lose our innocence to just *enjoy* things, and to allow God's love to bring *life* to all things.

Freedom in Being

Let's move to some reflection time. Think back to when you were within the age range of 5 to 10 years old. What was your personality like as a child? Take your time and think back to what your personality was like then. Write it here:

What were your interests? What did you enjoy doing? Write it here:

What our personalities were like as a child and the freedom we had appears to be a part of who we really are deep down. But as we get older and the world creeps in, we often mold into what everyone's expectations are for our personalities and lose some of that innocence. As we get older, we will mature and that is okay. Having a childlike faith does not mean being naive or not maturing. But I think we can learn a lot from children about freedom and freedom in *being*...

Do you experience freedom in *being* like a child does?

Safe with God

Who in your life right now do you feel emotionally safe with? Do you know what I mean by emotionally safe? I mean people who you can be yourself around the most and you know they won't see you any different. People who you can say anything that you're feeling and thinking and they'll love you just the same? People who you can be vulnerable and free with? Do you have a particular person or group of people in mind? Jot them down below:

My husband is one of the people I think of that I feel emotionally safe with. He has seen all sides of me. What's interesting is that I am the most like I was when I was a child when I'm around him. When I think back to that age range that I asked you to reflect on, I remember being goofy, creative, observant, abstract, and free. I find myself being those things when it's just him and I. Do you find yourself feeling free and childlike with who you wrote above?

Let's connect all of this to our relationship with God. These safe people that you described are a gift from *God*. Take the safety you feel with them and multiply it times a billion and that's the safety you can feel with God. God uses his people to show a glimpse of his overwhelming love for each of us.

We can have complete security that our Father loves us. (We can feel fully safe with him). We can have innocence like a child when we are with him. He is always with us. We can have that innocence all the time if we allow our security to be in God.

What is your security in? Is it in a person? Your family? Your career? Something else? Going back to the very beginning of the book, if someone were to ask you: Who are you? Would you answer it based on what you do? Or would you say:

> *I am a child of God. And my worth, security, and*
> *hope is based on God being my Father….*

God desires for our security to be in him. But maybe having our security in God doesn't have to look like what we thought it looked like? Maybe it doesn't have to be filled with only Christian "stuff" and instead can be filled with experiencing God through all things and the way he created us? Sounds pretty freeing to me, how about you?

To close this chapter, enter into the experience below about a woman who is experiencing *freedom in all things…*

It's 7:00AM, my alarm is buzzing, and a new day begins. I wonder what today will hold. I grab the Bible next to my bed and begin the day with studying Scripture. As I meditate on it, I find the Lord breathing life into my time with him and feel refreshed for the day.

I slow down to enjoy and cook a breakfast with eggs, hashbrowns, and a glass of orange juice. I read the morning newspaper and complete a crossword. I find the Lord breathing life into enjoying my breakfast and resting to start the day. I take a quick shower and am feeling awake.

I go to wake up my little girl, Faith. She smiles at me and says "Morning, Mommy." I find the Lord breathing life into my day through the way my daughter looks at me.

She takes a quick bath and we are ready to start the day. We head to the supermarket and I begin to check off my list the items that are needed. We get up to pay and the cashier appears to be having a bad day. I smile at her and thank her for her help and she smiles back at me. I felt the Lord breathing life into her through my smile.

On our drive home, I put on the local Christian radio station, and worship God through a song I love that they often play on the station. As the song ends, I switch the dial to a country station and Faith and I begin to dance a little because the station also has on one of my favorite songs. I find the Lord breathing life into our car through both genres of music.

We get home, eat lunch, and I decide to go with Faith for a walk around the neighborhood. I gaze at the beauty of the trees, plants, flowers, and sky around me. I feel so at peace being outside and I find God breathing life into our time in his creation.

When we get back from our walk, Faith insists on watching her favorite movie. I watch her laugh and her eyes light up from time to time during the movie. I find the Lord breathing life through the innocence of my little girl.

As the day begins to wind down, my husband gets home from a long day at work. As soon as he walks in the door, he wraps me in his arms with a hug. I tell him I love him and he tells me he loves me too. I find God breathing life through the love my husband has for me.

Faith, him and I enjoy dinner together and we share about our days. We share with each other, laugh with each other, and simply love each other. I find God breathing life through the quality time we have spent together as a family.

We head into the family room to finish up the night. My husband looks at me and asks "did you experience the Lord today in any way?" I smile at him and looked back on my day. Before I can respond, Faith answers with "Yes daddy. We saw Jesus at the supermarket, on our walk, in the car, when we were watching a movie, at dinner, and he is still with us now." I smiled at her and my husband and said, "She's right, he breathed life into every part of our day."

Chapter 3 Reflection Questions

1. What do you feel when you hear the word "safe?" What or who comes to your mind?

2. In what areas in your life do you find yourself experiencing freedom?

3. Where or with whom in your life do you find yourself being childlike? Do you feel childlike in your relationship with God?

CHAPTER 4 ~ The Condition of the Heart

*No one has ever seen God. But the unique One, who is Himself God, **is near to the Father's heart**. He has revealed God to us.*
~John 1:18 (NLT)

When I was in college, I worked at a Christian campground in Ohio. Our program director was also like a spiritual mentor to all of us working there and I remember one day him calling us into his office. He did this often when God would put something on his heart to share with us. He said that God had been teaching him that everything in this life comes back to the *condition of the heart*.

At the time, I didn't fully understand what the "condition of the heart" meant, but it has become more clear. Let's think about the word "condition." It's kind of like the state that something is in.

In the Ebay world when you list an item, you are asked to describe the "condition" of the item. The options include: brand new, like new, very good, good, acceptable, and poor. And then you sell the item based on its condition. A brand new item is most likely going to sell for more than an item in poor condition. So the condition of the item often affects the value of the item.

Another way to think about a condition is to think about a "grade" of an old baseball card. Vintage baseball cards are often sent out to different companies to be professionally graded. Grades are on a scale of 1 to 10. 1 is considered "poor to fair condition" and 10 is considered "gem mint" condition. Often the grade of a vintage baseball card could affect its value by hundreds of dollars. So again, the condition of the card affects the value of the card.

When it comes to our lives, the condition of our *heart* affects everything. Have you ever been around someone whose heart is bitter and resentful? When you're around someone like that for a long period of time, all of a sudden you find yourself feeling bitter and resentful. Have you ever been around someone who is full of hope, peace, and contentment? Somehow just being around them brings you hope. The condition of our hearts will affect our relationship with God, family, friends, and ourselves. Everything in this life comes back to the condition of the heart.

> **The condition of our heart affects everything**

Backwards

It seems that we often get things backwards when it comes to following God. We often preach and teach on "changing behaviors" instead of searching the condition of our hearts. When the condition of our hearts is in a place of wholeness, trust, and healing in God- we naturally want to change and follow his commands. But when the condition of our hearts is in a place of baggage, fear, hurt, or anger toward God, it will be difficult for us to change our behaviors because deep down we may not fully trust him.

Let's use an example of a human relationship. Imagine walking down a road and meeting a random person for the first time who tells you a list of things he wants you to do for him. You would probably think something like "No, that's crazy, I don't even know you!" You don't *know* the person, you haven't *experienced* a relationship with them, and you haven't built *trust* in that person. This same concept seems to happen within church walls. We learn command after command of behaviors we need to change in our life without hearing an emphasis on *knowing* this God that we're told to follow. As we *experience* this God's heart, *experience* his presence, as we get to *know* this God's heart for us, and *trust* is built in our relationship with him- it is then that we want to serve him.

Following God is a direct response from our heart condition knowing, experiencing, and trusting in him.

The greatest commandment in the Word says to love the Lord your God with all your *heart*, soul, and mind. The *second* is to love your neighbor as yourself (Matthew 22: 34-40, NLT). There is a specific order used here. God confirms in these Scriptures the importance of focusing on our heart condition *first* and then serving others.

If you think back on your life, when do you remember *experiencing* God? How did that experience affect your trust in him?

He wants your heart

One of the things that I really struggle with in my heart condition is feeling the need to perform. This includes the need to perform for others and to perform for God. One night I came home and was really struggling with performing in writing this book. I was feeling overwhelmed by wanting to meet every reader's expectations instead of being obedient to God's expectations. I got down on my knees and asked the Lord, what would you have me write? As I asked him that question, I felt my heart feeling so worn down in trying to perform and meet expectations. I spent some time being still and sensed his small, silent voice speaking:

"Stacy, I want **your** heart. I care more about your heart being free than anything you could *do* for me...."

My eyes were immediately filled with tears, and I felt so overwhelmed with God's love for *me*. Not because of anything I *do* for him or areas I try to perform in, but because of his heart for my heart. He cared more about my heart being free and healed then anything else. He desires the same for you. Please allow the statement below to flood your heart:

> *God cares more about the condition of your heart being*
> *free and healed than anything you could **do** for him.*

Completely His

Do you need a heart transplant? Not in the physical sense, but in the spiritual sense. What does the condition of your heart look like? Is it healthy and filled with trust toward God? Or is it filled with memories of disappointment with God, others, and yourself? As we will discuss in a later chapter, often what we go through in life will affect the condition of our hearts.

Think of healing your heart in comparison to healing a physical sickness. If you are sick, you go to the doctor and they will give you a diagnosis. So they will search for the underlying issue that is making you feel sick. Then, the doctor will most likely give you medicine to help heal the sickness over time.

That is a similar process to how we deal with healing our hearts. First, we figure out what is making our heart feel so much pain, worry, regret, etc. Once we have identified that, then we go to God as our doctor, and allow him to give us the medicine of his love and his wisdom to help us heal from the pain over time.

Depending on the depth of the pain, you may need to seek out someone you trust to help you through the process of healing as well. This may be a close friend, a mentor, pastor, or professional counselor. God can speak through them to help you through the process if you are feeling overwhelmed.

I wonder what Jesus would see if he sat in the back of our church services. I truly believe that Jesus sees the condition of our heart above all else. If he were to sit in the back pew, and watch people worship- he wouldn't see who was raising their hands and who wasn't. He wouldn't see who was paying attention and who wasn't. He wouldn't see what people were wearing or who was sitting next to who. He would see *heart conditions*. As he scans the service, these are some of the things he might see:

*A heart with chains of bondage around it

*A heart that is free, healthy, and filled with love

*A heart that is filled with dirt, sin, and guilt

*A heart that is heavy

*A heart burdened with unforgiveness and resentment

*A heart that is hurting

* a heart filled with fear

*A heart that is content

*A heart thirsty for more of God

*A broken heart

*A heart with walls around it

The following verse describes the condition of the heart God desires for his people:

For the eyes of the Lord move to and fro throughout the Earth, that He may strongly support those whose heart is completely His...
~2 Chronicles 16:9 (NASB)

Wow, read that verse over again if you need to. The condition of the heart that God desires is the condition of being "Completely His." He desires for us to find our identity in being completely his.

Completely His...

Shifting Our Focus

Have you ever noticed that it often seems that God doesn't allow things to fall into place in our lives until our heart is fully his? I've experienced this personally and watched it happen time and time again in other individuals. In those times when we have an important decision to make in our lives, we wait for God to open and close doors. We are waiting for him to reveal to us what that next step is. But instead, we hear silence. And the silence can be frustrating. *Often, the silence is because he wants us to shift our focus to our heart conditions.* The silence can be a way to refocus our minds on God and allow him to change the condition of our heart. When we allow our hearts to be completely his, it is then that things seem to fall into place.

What would the Lord see if he were to look at your heart today? What would it look like? If the condition of your heart is not in a place of being completely his, it is okay. Yes, it is okay… Go to God with that. Don't cover your heart up and try to act like everything is okay. Open it up to God and to others who love you and allow yourself to get a heart transplant. It will be a process. This is so important because the condition of our heart will affect what our identity is in and our ability to accept all that God has for us as his children.

More than anything, there is one thing that God's eyes search for….a heart that is completely his.

Completely His…

To close this chapter, I encourage you to take a look at the heart below. Within the drawing, draw or write words that describe what the condition of your heart looks like today:

Chapter 4 Reflection Questions

1. If Jesus' eyes were searching your heart right now, what would he see?

2. "He cares more about the condition of your heart being free and healed than anything you could *do* for him."
   ~What did you feel and think when reading this?

3. If you don't feel like your heart is completely his, what steps can you take to move in that direction?

CHAPTER 5 ~ Balance

Take a look at the line below:

●---●

Think of this line with the right dot at the end of the line being one extreme of Christian thinking and the other dot as being the other extreme. In the last ten years I've trotted from one extreme to another in search of finding a sense of peace in my heart. I've been exposed to a variety of different denominations of churches. So I've been exposed to churches on a lot of different points on that line. Some churches seem to be based on one extreme of "grace" and others on "works." Some seem to be based on "struggles/hardships" and on the other end of the line "prosperity." Some appear to take nothing literal in the Bible while others take everything literal in the Bible.

I cannot tell you that I've found the "correct" denomination and that's not what this book is about anyways. And maybe there isn't a "correct" denomination? I can tell you though that

I personally have found peace in the middle of this line, in a place of balance.

What if there is a time and a place for everything? What if there is a time for grace and time for works, a time for struggles and a time for prosperity, a time to not take things literally and a time to take them literally? What if there is a balance in between?

> *For everything there is a season, A time for every activity under heaven. A time to be born and a time to die. A time to plant and a time to harvest. A time to kill and a time to heal. A time to tear down and a time to build up. A time to cry and a time to laugh. A time to grieve and a time to dance. A time to scatter stones and a time to gather stones. A time to embrace and a time to turn away. A time to search and a time to quit searching. A time to keep and a time to throw away. A time to tear and a time to mend. A time to be quiet and a time to speak. A time to love and a time to hate. A time for war and a time for peace.*
> *~Ecclesiastes 3:1-8 (NLT)*

Let's think about the life of a child for a second. One of the first things I think of when I think of children is a sense of simplicity. A movie recently came out called "Letters to God." It is about a little boy who has cancer who writes a letter to God every day and puts it in the mailbox. As his life draws near to an end, he ends up inspiring hundreds of people to begin writing their own letters to God. As the credits were rolling at the end of the movie, my husband looked over at me and said:

"I can't stop thinking about how simple his letters were. He wrote about being mad at his brother, helping other people, and he was just real. He didn't say "Dear God, thou art great.

32

Blesseth my body and health. Grant us wisdom. Thou art Holy."

There seems to be a lot of pressure within church walls for people to be more "spiritual" than others. There can be pressure to impress one another, out-serve each other, and to have it all together. At times, we ask the question that the disciples in the first Scripture we looked at in this book asked. "Who is the greatest?" Jesus pulled a little child and said become like this little child.

Another thing I love about working with children is observing their imagination and the way they look at things. Children seem to live for two things: love and play. They love to feel loved and they love to play. They love to play because they can use their imagination and create things.

Do we focus on love and play in our lives? Or do we focus on legalism and rules? I want to add here a reminder of balance. Rules and commands are not bad things. We just have to make sure they don't become our *main focus* or *identity*. Our identity is in being a child of God. From that identity, we then serve and follow his commands in response to that love. Love brings a desire to serve the One you love..

Check Your Gut

Do you ever have a gut feeling about something? Like this overwhelming feeling deep down in your gut that is hard to ignore? The only way I can think of describing this "gut" feeling is that it will either bring a sense of "this is right on" or "this is off." Your gut feeling is something to listen to in every area of life. For the purpose of this book we are going to focus on your gut feeling when it comes to balance within Christianity.

Have you ever heard a teaching, read a book, or had a conversation with someone where your gut was screaming

33

inside of you "this is off!" One way to check whether something is bringing a sense of balance in your heart is what it makes you feel. Is what is being taught or said bringing a sense of guilt, shame, or condemnation? Or is it bringing a sense of peace, conviction, and freedom? God is not the author of condemnation, guilt, or shame but he is the author of peace, conviction, and freedom. This is a good way to decipher if you are hearing a balanced perspective or not.

Gray Area

One thing I've noticed as I've journeyed back and forth along the line pictured at the beginning of this chapter is that it's easier for us at times to look at things from a black and white perspective than to explore the realms of possibilities in there being a gray area. Scripture is filled with talk of someone called the Holy Spirit. He is abstract and free and reveals personal things to specific people that he doesn't reveal to others. He revealed to Mary that she was going to give birth to Jesus, yet she was a virgin? In the Word he never revealed to any other virgin that they were going to give birth to a child who would become the King? That doesn't seem very black and white- it seems abstract and an individual conviction for Mary specifically (a gray area).

On the other hand, you read in Scripture other commands that seem to be very black and white. For example, do not commit adultery. Do not judge. So is Christianity a black and white religion or is there a gray area? What I'm learning in this process is that there appears to be both.

Have you ever noticed that theological arguments and debates tend to never get anywhere except causing division between the relationships of the people arguing? Maybe there is a reason for that. It seems that a lot of times people are trying to make gray area issues black and white. Everyone has certain convictions, but one person's conviction may be different than the person sitting next to them.

I want to note here that gray areas are not things that *we* create. There can be a tendency to create gray areas on our own to feel more comfortable. Gray areas are specific, individual convictions that *God* has given you.

At this point I began to write a list of areas that God has shown me are gray areas in my life and areas that are black and white. Then I deleted them because I want you as the reader, to take a minute and really reflect on this concept for yourself. See if the Holy Spirit wants to show you your own areas of black and white, and gray. If so, write them below in the chart provided. Below the chart are some examples to help you understand the differences between the two.

Black and White Areas (Absolutes)	Gray Areas (Individual/ Personal Convictions)
1.	
2.	
3.	

*Black and White/Absolutes- These are areas that are absolutes for everyone within Christianity. For example, an absolute might be "Do not steal. Do not be drunk. "

*Gray Areas/Individual Convictions- These are individual convictions that God has shown you personally that may be different for you than others. An example for this one is "do not have more than one glass of wine."

When I began to learn this concept, it was so freeing to me. I found myself feeling like a child again in a way, and feeling a freedom that I hadn't felt before. I began to "love and play" like children do. At times we can get so caught up in "Christian stuff" and legalistic rules that we begin to miss knowing *God* Himself.

So I pose this reflection question to us- are we living a life of love and play? Or are we following a set of rules that a church or people have set for us instead of God and Scripture? Where do you fall on this line below and where do you want to be?

●--●

Chapter 5 Reflection Questions

1. How do you feel about the concept of balance?

2. What areas did you find that were black and white areas in your life? What areas did you find that were gray?

3. Are your convictions based on what others would think of them, what you've been taught, or on what God has specifically revealed to you?

CHAPTER 6 ~ Uniquely You

Few are those who see with their own eyes
and feel with their own hearts.
~Albert Einstein

How did God uniquely create you? It is amazing that no one person is the same physically, mentally, or emotionally. There are specific similarities that you can find between two individuals but they will never be exactly the same. God designed it that way for a purpose. It's important in this process of finding your identity in God that you find out how God uniquely created you specifically.

Have you ever noticed how emotion is brought out when someone is vulnerable with their own unique story? When someone sings a song and you can feel the emotion behind it when they're singing- it moves you. Many of the great movies of our time are based on true stories. These movies aren't fictional and created- they are based on real people's struggles and stories. Reality television ratings have skyrocketed. Viewers tend to identity themselves with someone in the show. Why do these avenues bring such emotion?

It seems that what the American church is thirsty for today is for vulnerability and stories that they can relate to. There is a thirst for transparency and the opportunity for people to be where they are. There is a thirst to get "real" and get rid of the fake.

The main concept of this chapter is the importance of being who God uniquely created you to be. There is freedom in being vulnerable with exactly where you are in your journey.

In the struggles and victories in this life- be raw, vulnerable, and uniquely you. There will be a sense of freedom that follows. Embrace and be vulnerable with who *you* are, where *you* are, and how God uniquely created *you*.

****

Here are a few of the differences between God's people:

Personality Types
Learning Styles
Spiritual Gifts
Love Languages

There is a beauty in how creatively God made each of us. It seems that at times we struggle with finding our identity because we are focused on what others expectations are for our identity. So we mold into what others molds are for us and never feel free.

Even within some church buildings, we often find "business" type structures and systems instead of the freedom and vulnerability in being sons and daughters of God. At times, these systems create spiritual "clones." When this happens, we miss out on the opportunity to experience freedom in how God uniquely created each of us. Often in these church bodies where we should be finding ourselves it is easy to "lose ourselves" in expectations. We can even lose our ability to think for ourselves at times.

Children are so unique and free. They "find themselves" through love and play as we talked about earlier. There is nothing complicated about who they are, they have the ability to simply *be*.

> What makes your heart feel free?

If you want to find out what God's call is in your life and are searching for who you are created to be, here is a simple question:

What makes your heart feel free?

Find the answer to that question first. If you feel your call is in something that doesn't make your heart feel free, then really pray and ask God if that is your calling. Keep in mind that what makes your heart feel free may not always be comfortable or easy. Your biggest gift is often your biggest struggle.

When I think of finding something that makes your heart feel free, I think of the word *peace*. Peace is not just a feeling, it is a heart condition. Peace directly comes from a heart that is completely God's. What makes you feel filled with God's peace? The next few sections of this chapter will break down some of the main differences between God's people. Hopefully you will discover more about who God uniquely created you to be.

Personality Types

What is your personality type? Throughout the internet, you can find hundreds of personality inventories to find out specifics about your personality. Are you extraverted or introverted? Are you energized when being around groups of people (extraverted) or drained when being in big groups of people (introverted)? Do you make decisions from more of an emotional/sensing standpoint or from a more logical standpoint?

Understanding your personality type can help you understand the way you process things, the way you see things, and why you may struggle with the things you struggle with. (It may be helpful to use an internet search engine and search for personality inventories if you want to explore more about your personality type.) God created you with your personality for a specific reason. How would you describe your personality? Write it here:

What has God showed you about your personality? Write it here:

Learning Style

Your learning style is based on the way you learn. Teachers often base their teaching techniques on the different learning styles within their class. Three common terms that break down learning styles include visual, auditory, and kinesthetic. We discussed earlier how different people experience God in different ways. Learning styles may play a big role in this.

Auditory learners learn best when they can physically hear something. Within Christianity, these types of learners may learn best through a sermon, teaching, or hearing people talk about their relationship with God. Auditory learners may not get as much out of reading or visually seeing something.

Kinesthetic learning styles are those who learn more from hands-on activities. So actually carrying out an activity helps them to learn. Within Christianity, listening to a sermon may be difficult for a kinesthetic to learn by. However, doing a bible study with a workbook may help them learn.

The final learning style is visual. These types of learners tend to organize things in their mind through images, pictures, colors, etc. They tend to process through visualizing. Within Christianity, this learning style may include those who enjoy painting or drawing.

What is your learning style? Write it here:

How does that style affect how you experience God? Write it here:

Spiritual Gifts

Spiritual Gifts are something discussed often within church bodies. There are tons of different spiritual gifting inventories. If you go online, you can find many different ones that can be helpful.

However, I am going to go a different direction in this book on spiritual gifts. One of my friends took a spiritual gifts inventory and was surprised at the results. She specifically scored high in the area of encouragement, and made an interesting comment. She said she didn't realize that she was using encouragement because it was so natural to her. She said it was as natural to her as breathing. Here is a way to look at your spiritual gifts:

Gifts come as natural to you as breathing...

If you are forcing yourself to use a gift, then it's not a gift. A gift is fluent and natural, not forced. In what ways have you noticed God using you? You may or may not have a "name" for the gift, just allow him to use you in that way.

Love Languages

Love Languages are based on a concept written by Gary Chapman in the book "The 5 Love Languages." The concept is often used for marriage purposes, but can be used for any relationship. It is based on the concept that there are five primary ways that we receive love from one another. These ways are considered "love languages."

Everyone has a love language. You may have one or more than one. The different love languages include Words of Affirmation, Quality Time, Acts of Service, Physical Touch, and Receiving Gifts. These different love languages help people identify how they give and receive love.

For example, let's pretend that a woman named Sarah has the love language of receiving gifts. Her husband, Bob could give Sarah tons of hugs (physical touch) and spend time with her (quality time), and it wouldn't mean as much to her as receiving a gift. Let's say Bob's love language is words of affirmation. Sarah could spend a lot of time with Bob and buy him a gift, and it wouldn't mean as much to him as if she verbally affirmed him.

Love Languages are powerful. They help you understand who you are as a child of God and how you receive love. It also can help you understand others in relationships based on their love language. If you visit www.5lovelanguages.com, you can learn more about the different love languages and take assessments to find out what your love language is.

Do you still dream?

Have you ever asked a child what their biggest dream is? The responses are amazing. You often will hear things like them wanting to be a pro sports player, a veterinarian, a doctor, or a fireman. Children don't limit their dreams, they just dream.

> *Jesus looked at them and said, "With man this is impossible, but with God all things are possible."*
> *~Matthew 19:26 (NIV)*

Let's take a look at the way the verse is worded. "With man this is impossible." I'm wondering if the word "man" is not necessarily referring to others but to ourselves. If we try to pursue a dream on our own strength, our own ability, and through our own ways- it will be *impossible*. But if we allow *God* to make the dream come alive, *all* things will be possible.

Do we truly believe this verse or is this verse only for young children who dream big? Dreams aren't always something that will touch millions of people. Your dream may only touch your small corner of the world or even just *you*. No matter who your dream touches, it is *worth* pursuing.

Allow this concept to sink into your spirit:

God has a
specific dream
for your life

What did you feel emotionally when reading that concept? As we get older, it seems that we lose our ability to *dream*. Does our Heavenly Father place an individual dream in each of his children's hearts? Do we allow that dream to be awakened or do we silence the dream when we feel it begin to surface? Often it seems that our dreams will be based on a combination of our personality types, learning styles, love languages, and spiritual gifts.

We discussed earlier about Jesus sitting in the back of a church service and searching for hearts that are completely his. Something that may grieve him is when he looks at hearts and finds this:

A dream that he has placed in a heart that has withered away

There are a variety of reasons why a dream may have withered away. Here are a few:

Fear*Disappointment* Lack of Confidence*Wanting Control*Insecurities*Unbelief*Life Circumstances

If there is a dream that God has placed on your heart, you may feel God awakening it, even right now as you are reading. If he is awakening a dream, describe the dream here:

When you feel him awakening it, do you feel yourself pushing it away? It is important to really examine our hearts and see what is holding us back from letting the dream awaken and pursuing it.

Below is a list of a variety of statements that may be running through your mind on why you may feel that you can't pursue your dream. Take a moment and circle the reason that resonates in you:

*It's too late to pursue my dream.

*Dreams aren't realistic in this world
and economy we're living in.

* What if I pursue my dream and fail?

*I have too many insecurities to feel confident in my dream.

*It's too much of a risk to pursue my dream.

*I don't believe that my dream can actually come true.

*I'm afraid of what could happen if I pursue my dream.

*If none of those statements are what is holding you back
from your dream, write one in below that you are thinking:

Spend some time in prayer with God about your dream. Share with him exactly what you are feeling and thinking, he already knows. Then spend some time listening about what he may want to show you.

A Specific Call

Within Scripture, God reveals specific callings to specific people. Take a look at the chart below:

Individual in Scripture	Specific Call
Noah	To build a boat and have his family enter into it. To bring a pair of every kind of animal and food to survive. After the flood took place, he was told to be fruitful and multiply. (Genesis 6:9-9:28)
Jeremiah	To warn the people of Judah and Jerusalem of the upcoming judgement of God because of worshipping idols and not following the Mosaic covenant (Book of Jeremiah)
Moses	Sent to perform miraculous signs and wonders in the land of Egypt against Pharaoh, Pharaoh's servants, and his land (Deuteronomy 34:11)
Nathan	Told by God in a vision to relay a specific message to David (2 Samuel 7: 1-17)

Daniel	God allowed Daniel to have experiences and visions that would teach God's people lessons about the kingdom of God (Book of Daniel)
Jonah	To go to Ninevah and announce God's judgment against it because of their wickedness (Jonah 1:1)
You	What is God's Call in your individual life?

So it seems that God uses specific individuals to portray a specific message. Notice the emphasis of the word *specific*. God created each of us so uniquely to communicate a unique message. All the people in this chart were children of God with a specific call based on the way God uniquely created them. *You* are a child of God and have a specific call based on the way God created *you*.

God sometimes has his people communicate a *verbal* message, however there are several books in the Bible where the word God is never or rarely mentioned and he is still glorified. So there is a *nonverbal* message about God sent as well (Example: The book of Esther). Is the message God is calling you to communicate verbal, nonverbal, or both?

For example, let's say you are a teacher and you are legally never able to say the word, God. You can communicate God's love through teaching without ever saying his name. You would have a *nonverbal* calling. If you are a church youth group leader you may have a *verbal* calling to speak of God's love to young people. If you are a stay-at-home mom your calling may be to raise your children up in the Lord. Your call will often be based on the unique way God created you and the specific gifts he has given you.

If you noticed at the end of the chart there was a space for "you." To close this chapter, reflect on being uniquely you. What is God's call on your life? What is the specific message God wants you to communicate? Fill in the "you" section of the chart below:

You	What is God's unique call on my life? What is the specific message he wants me to communicate:

Chapter 6 Reflection Questions

1. Based on what you've read, how would you describe your personality type, learning style, spiritual gifts, and love language?

2. Is there a dream that you feel God may be awakening in your life? If so, how would put the dream into words?

3. How would you describe your call and the message God would have for you to communicate? Do you have a verbal or nonverbal calling? Or Both?

CHAPTER 7 ~ Pour it Out...

"The sacrifices of God are a broken Spirit;
a broken and contrite heart."
~Psalm 51:17 (KJV)

What do you believe about who God is? Answer this question from a heart standpoint, not just a logical standpoint. What do you *really* believe about God? Do you trust him? Do you *really* trust him? Do you believe that he is good? Do you *really* believe that he is good? Is there anything about God that you know in your mind but are having trouble really believing in your heart? If so, write it below:

What you go through in your past often affects how you view God now. For example, if you had a father who left you, you may struggle with a fear that God may abandon you. If you went through abuse of any kind, you may struggle with God being a protector. You may have gone through something recently or currently. For example, losing a job or loved one. Every situation is different, but I would encourage you to really examine how what you've been through or are going through affects what you believe about God.

I know that the concept that what you go through in your life transfers onto what you believe about God is controversial. My prayer is that you will at least be open to exploring with God if something you have gone through is connected in any way. The reason I encourage this concept, is because I have experienced it personally and have seen it take place with others. Let me share an example from my personal journey.

I have experienced several episodes of severe depression. As you may know, when you go through depression you often lose motivation, feel extremely sad, and are easily fatigued. You also often struggle with feeling alone. When I went through these times, I felt like God didn't hear my prayers. I remember wanting so badly for the depression to be over, so I could experience what other teenagers got to experience, but it stayed for long periods of time. I remember begging the Lord to get me out of it, and nothing changed. So for a long time, I struggled with the following concept:

Does God really care about my heart? If he really did, why would he allow me to go through this so many times at such a young age?

This belief became rooted deeply in my heart until I went through counseling years later. I realized that what I believed about God not caring about my heart was a lie. It took me a long time to resolve. However, in time I began to believe again that God cares about my heart, even if I don't always understand his ways. My heart was beginning to heal from the hurt.

Here is another example from someone close to me who went through childhood sexual abuse. Starting at age 6, she was consistently raped by another adolescent until age 10. During this time period, she remembers sharing with a parent what was going on and them not believing her. She felt so hurt, disappointed, and let down that her parents didn't believe her.

Now, as an adult, she finds herself transferring those feelings onto God, because God is often described as a parental figure. (A father figure) She felt her parents weren't there for her, she couldn't feel safe with them, and they didn't protect her. So she often feels those same qualities are portrayed in God.

Being Real with Ourselves and with God

Are you real with God about hurt you may have? When a child is crying, a parent comforts them. Children don't hide pain like adults often do. As children of God, cry out to the Father and he will comfort you.

It's important that we are being honest with ourselves first before we can be honest with God. For example, let's imagine someone really hurt a girl name Sarah. Sarah has convinced herself that the hurt wasn't a big deal and didn't bother her that much. So there is an avoidance of acknowledging that hurt. Until Sarah is honest with herself about the depth of hurt that is there, she cannot be honest with God about it.

So the first step is to be honest with *ourselves* about hurt we may be feeling. The second step is to acknowledge it to *God*. The second step cannot take place without the first.

Take a moment and look at the image on the next page of a glass pitcher filled with water.

For the purpose of this chapter, this pitcher will be a visual of your heart. Water is sometimes filled with contaminants we don't see or acknowledge. From the outside they may not be noticeable. However, they can make you sick. The water inside of the pitcher will be symbolic of pain/hurt in your heart. This pain may include situations and circumstances in your life currently or it may include things from your past that you're having trouble letting go of. The water may be filled with resentment, bitterness, regret, anger, sadness, grief, etc.

If you were to describe what your pitcher (heart) would contain specifically in terms of pain, how would you describe it? Use the space below to describe it. Take your time:

Now, that you have identified what areas of pain are there, you have made it through the first step. The first step as described earlier is to be honest with ourselves and acknowledge the pain. The second step is to acknowledge it to God.

Before we move onto the second step, it's important to clarify that a lot of times people get *stuck* between the first and second step. There are a variety of reasons for this happening. One is that it's too painful to acknowledge the pain to God. It *hurts* to deal with pain. But, the pain that you will experience in pouring out your hurt to God can't compare with the **freedom** that you will experience when you release it.

Another thing that holds people back from acknowledging pain to God or to others is that we want to put a lid on the pitcher. In other words, we want to be *guarded* with the pain. We don't want to let anyone in. We may have gotten hurt before by letting someone in, so we're afraid of getting hurt again. God created us for *relationship*, relationship with him and relationship with others. So, we can't just put a lid on our heart and expect to experience freedom.

So using the visualization of the pitcher, pour out the pain to him through prayer. When water is pouring out of a pitcher it is fluid and natural. So when you share it with him, don't analyze what you are saying, *just pour it out.*

If you feel led, put this book away and pour out your heart to God, even right now. Remember there is no formula for this, just be honest with yourself and with God.

Pour the pain out to God

There may be a close person in your life who you feel led to pour it out to as well. It may be a spouse, close friend, pastor, or counselor.

After you have poured it out, spend some time *listening*. We discussed earlier how listening for God is often something that is put to the side. After you pour out the pain, pray and ask God if there is anything he would want to show you, and then listen. He may speak something specific to you or you may simply feel his comfort.

Once you have poured it out and spent time listening, God desires to replace the water that has been poured out. It is replaced with pure, new water. He wants to renew and refresh the pain you experienced with peace.

I feel the need to add here that these steps may not be instantaneous. It may happen suddenly, instantly. It may take hours, days, weeks, or months. There is no time constraint on the process. The important thing is asking God to help you with whatever the next step may be.

Restoration of Innocence

You rarely see a little child questioning God, doubting God, or not trusting God. If I were to ask a child the same question posed at the beginning of this chapter, what do you *really* believe about God? They would most likely genuinely be able to say I love God and I believe that he loves me. Why is that? Why as we get older does it get harder and harder to have a simple faith? Usually children are sheltered from harm, hurt, and the world

58

around them as much as possible until they are at an age where they can understand. What if God can restore a pure, childlike innocence even in a world of pain and struggle? What if?

Have you ever observed a baby when they're sleeping in their mom or dad's arms? They seem so peaceful and content. They *trust* their mom and dad and *rest* in knowing that they will take care of them. As they grow older and begin to talk and communicate, everything their parents say is reality. Whatever the parent teaches them is truth in their mind. As they continue to get older and begin to experience the pain and heartache in this world, they lose that innocence and often begin to question this world and this God that created them. As we experience this life and the pain and heartache it brings, can we still *trust* this God? This *Father?* Life isn't about hiding or avoiding the pain. It's about letting life happen, and seeking to understand God more through it all...

Being a counselor, I've been able to see people experience their worst nightmares first hand. When I first began in this profession, I questioned God. I wondered what it would be like, if my worst nightmare happened to me. At first, I tried avoiding the questions. But then, I tackled the questions and tried to understand God more through them. And what I found.... something *beautiful.*

I began to meditate on the verse that promises that God will give us a peace that transcends our own understanding. Not a peace that we create on our own, but a peace that transcends all of our own understanding, a peace that only *God* could give. So even if our greatest fear takes place, we will still have *God.* We will still have *everything.* The Holy Spirit will work on our behalf to help us through our most difficult times.

This doesn't mean that if you are going through a difficult struggle in your life right now, that it will be easy. It also doesn't mean that you can't have questions, doubt, and disappointment.

It means that there is a God who will pursue you with his peace amidst the questions, doubt, and disappointment. And who will never stop pursuing you...

So again, I continue to pose this question before you continue reading. What do you believe about God? This is important to sort through before you continue on with this book. Because the circumstances and situations you've gone through in your life may create lies about who God is. By identifying lies that you believe first and where they came from, it will help you compare as you read to the truth of who God is as our Father. And who we are as his children.

A Letter from Your Father:

For this next experience, visualize this letter as a letter that Your Heavenly Father has written you. This letter is based on biblical concepts. If you feel comfortable, write a letter back to God in response. Remember, we talked about God being an approachable Father, so don't hold back. Allow this letter to flood your soul with Abba's love for you:

My Child,

You can trust me. You can really trust me. You may not be able to understand it all, but you can trust me fully like a child. I desire to restore in you the innocence of a child, even with what you've been through. I'm your Father, Abba, your Papa. I've never left you and never will. I desire to hold you like a little baby in my arms, while you rest in me.

Can you let go of the pain and trust me again? If you're not ready, it's okay. I'll be waiting patiently until you are ready. If you're ready, Come. Come, let me hold you, my child...Rest in me.

*Oh, if you could only fully comprehend how much I love you. I desire so much for you. I desire for you to grow in love in every aspect of your life here on this Earth- that you may grow in love toward others, yourself, and in my love. But, you see, you can't fully love until you allow my love to fully come alive in you. For that to happen, you have to let me in...and to let me in... You have to **trust** me. Really **trust** me, not just say it....*

Trust that I am good.

Trust that I am God.

Trust that I have your best interests at heart, even if you can't understand it all.

I have promised you that I will never leave you alone. I have promised that if you let me in, I will give you life and life abundantly. Life abundantly doesn't mean a perfect life that is free from pain and disappointment. Life abundantly is a promise that you will receive everything I have for you and that I will put your best interests at heart. Life abundantly is a promise that I will use all things for the good.

*What is holding you back from fully trusting me and believing that I am good? What is holding you back from **being** and allowing me to be God?*

Chapter 7 Reflection Questions

1. What comes to your mind personally when thinking of how things we go through can transfer onto what we believe about God?

2. If there is something on your heart that you feel like you need to pour out- spend some time writing a letter back to God (Just like writing a letter to a close friend). Express any hurt you may be feeling when you think back in the past or currently.

CHAPTER 8 ~ Foundation in Our Father

"For all who are led by the Spirit of God are children of God.
So you have not received a spirit that makes you fearful slaves.
Instead you received God's Spirit when He adopted you as
His own children. Now we call Him, "Abba, Father."
~Romans 8:14-15 (NLT)

As we've been discovering about what it means to be a child of God, it's important for us to discover as well what it means for God to be our Father. Who is this Father? Who is this God who we call Abba? Is he like an earthly Father or is he different? What is he like?

I began a search to find an answer to these questions. I tried to block everything I've "heard" or "learned" about God and strictly looked at Scripture. I began to study the attributes that God is described as. Here is what I found:

God is:
*Eternal
*Good
*Our Heavenly Father

*Not Limited
*All-Powerful
*Self-Sufficient
*Sovereign
*Just
*All-Knowing
*Never Changing
*Holy
*Always Present
*Trustworthy
* *Love*

These are just a few of the many attributes of God. As I studied these attributes, I began to take a step back and compare these attributes to what I struggle with putting my identity in. No identity I could find could compare with the attributes of God. Our families, careers, physical appearances, friendships, and no amount of money can compare with the promises, attributes, and love of God.

I feel the need to emphasize here that it is important to remember that there is a distinct separation between God and man. God is Holy, *set apart* (Isaiah 6:3). There needs to be a balance between viewing God as a nurturing friend type of relationship and a Holy God who is in a place of authority. There needs to be a balance between *relationship* and *reverence to a Holy God.* Do you struggle more with seeing God as a friend or a Holy God?

As these concepts began to sink in, I began to visualize a heart. In this heart, there was one section that only God could fill. *Only* Him. *No other identity will satisfy the part of our hearts that only God can fill.* Nothing else will fit. No person, thing, or concept can fill our need for God.

Take a moment and think about the closest person to you in your life. Pick the person who knows you the most. Once you have that person in mind, allow this to sink in:

No person will ever be able to enter the space where God's love pours into.

The space where God enters his love into is intimate. It is a secret place set apart from all else for God and you. When that foundational space is filled with God's love it overflows into all other areas in your heart. It overflows into all other relationships, needs, and desires.

It's important that the foundation of our heart is filled with God alone. Once that foundation is set and secure, then it overflows into other areas that God created us for.

Trusting in Our Father

Our Father is *perfect*. If we have this perfect Father, why doesn't each person have full 100% trust in him? Based on all the promises and attributes described above, why wouldn't we fully trust this perfect Father? I believe that our lack of trust comes from three things:

1. Our life circumstances and what we've been through have taught us things about God that aren't true. (As discussed earlier)

2. We don't understand it **all**....

3. We're afraid of giving him <u>complete</u> control, and instead only want to give him some.

Our Father is a mysterious Father. He reveals things to us that we can understand and allows things to be mysteries that we can't understand. He tells us that his ways are higher than our ways and his thoughts higher than ours. So we may not understand his ways. It may be scary to truly give him complete control.

Take a moment and read back through the three reasons described earlier of why we struggle with trusting God. Do any of these resonate in your heart? If so, circle the reason and share it with God.

Risk

There is a lot to risk in trusting God as our Father. We are risking the possibility that God may allow us to go through something that feels terrible to us. We are risking the possibility of God taking someone in our family or someone we are extremely close to. We are risking the possibility of God saying "no" in an area where we want to hear "yes." Or "yes" in an area where we want to hear "no." We are risking the things we think we want and need for the things God wants for us, and the needs he wants to fulfill. We are *risking it all* to fully trust this Father. Sounds scary, doesn't it?

But here's the thing:

It is worth it. It is worth the risk.

I recently was reading a forum on a Christian web site with the following question posed as the topic: "Do you marry for love or do you marry because you're committed to that person?" In other words, "what role does commitment play in love?"

20 people posted replies to this question, and it was interesting to me the debate that arose from the question asked. The typical responses of the first 9 posts all involved discussing praying for God's will for your life, and finding someone with all the aspects of love described in the Bible, and how love is a decision and a choice. As I was reading these posts, I would agree that these things are true and those were the answers I would expect Christians to post on a Christian forum.

But then I got to the 10th post, and I was surprised at what I read. This writer went a different direction. He responded with: "everyone you love WILL eventually hurt you. Whether that be intentionally or unintentionally. The people you love the most will hurt you the most. How do you know if you want to marry someone? Are you willing to take all the pain you will receive for loving that person?

"Love is as much hurting as it healing. As much pain as it is wellness. As much sorrow as it joy. Love is not always returned the way we expect it to be, and sometimes it's not even returned at all. And that is the worst kind of pain you'll ever experience. So you need to ask yourself if you really are willing to endure the potential of all of this….If you are, that's unconditional love. And that's how you're ready for whatever the next step is."

Interesting response, isn't it? Take a guess at what the last 9 posts responded…with an uproar! They replied to this post with explaining how simple love and knowing God's will is, and throwing Bible verses and theological arguments at the one who posted.

I'm not going to address whether every part of that post was theologically sound or correct, but I am going to address the heart of what that person seemed to be trying to communicate about love. There were three statements that stuck out to me that were made by this writer.

1. The people you love the most will hurt you the most.
2. Love is as much hurting as healing.
3. Are you willing to endure the potential of all of this?

Let's rephrase this into one statement to apply to love in our relationship with God.

"The more you love God, the more possibility you have of experiencing hurt. Are you willing to take this risk?"

Take a moment, re-read, and ponder that statement.

The people we love the most, have the ability to hurt us the most because we are *letting them in* our hearts. So now we have *God*, who desires to be the most intimate person and being in our heart. When we *let him into* our hearts and begin to find our identity in him alone, he may allow us to go through hurt.

Love and pain cannot be separated on this Earth. They are one. You cannot have one without the other. And since God defines the fullness of love on this Earth, he also allows us to experience pain on this Earth. He may not directly "cause" the pain, but he will allow it to happen at times.

Most would agree that the question most posed to the church is "If God is good, then why does he allow pain?" I'm not going to answer that question for you, but instead pose an additional question. Why is this question asked more than any other by people? Is it because pain is the most sensitive and misunderstood topic to mankind? Think about this. Stepping into God's will for your life involves a series of choices. So every time you make a choice to align yourself with God's will, it's as if you are opening yourself up to a possibility to experience pain. You could be opening yourself up to the most sensitive and misunderstood mystery. You may experience the fullness of love, pain, or both. That is part of the risk.

God could allow you to feel the fullness of pain, if you follow him. How could you completely trust a love that may allow you to go through such pain? *Because there's more...*

God promised in His Word that he will allow us to experience pain. But he also promised that he will *bless* us and that we will never be alone. He promises us that he will give us a love that no other identity can give us. We are given every promise in His Word if we chose to *let him in.* Have you allowed him to enter into the most intimate place in your heart or is something holding you back? If so, what is holding you back?

A Solid Foundation

When you take this risk, you may not understand everything and it may be scary at times, but you can have assurance that your foundation is secure. Check this out:

I will show you what it's like when someone comes to Me, listens to My teaching, and then follows it. It is like a person digging a house who digs deep and lays the foundation on solid rock. When the floodwaters rise and break against that house, it stands firm because it is well built. But anyone who hears and doesn't obey is like a person who builds a house without a foundation. When the floods sweep down against that house, it will collapse into a heap of ruins.
~Luke 6: 47-49 (HCSB)

What is your foundation in? Is your foundation in man and how others perceive you? Is your foundation in your family? Is your foundation in your career? Is your foundation in your ministry and *doing* things for God? Is your foundation in financial security? Is your foundation in having control? Is it in you?

I feel the need to add here a reminder of what we focused on earlier about balance. Your family, ministry, etc. are not *bad things*. God speaks through so many different avenues. It's just remembering not to put your full *security* or *foundation* in them.

I struggle at times with putting my foundation in my career/ ministry since they are the same. In my career, if I feel rejection from someone or feel like I didn't meet someone's expectations, I have a really hard time. When I feel rejection, it is like a river is crashing against the foundation of my house, and it collapses. However, there is something that helps me with this struggle. When I feel like I'm not meeting an expectation, I remind myself of this concept:

> *I am a child of God. And my worth, security, and*
> *hope is based on God being my Father....*

As I allow that concept to resonate in my Spirit, I feel free and secure in myself. I feel safe. I feel like I cannot be shaken. I feel *loved* in a way that is indescribable.

> *For where your treasure is, there your heart will be also.*
> *~Luke 12:34 (NIV)*

If you're having trouble identifying what your foundation is in, ask yourself the following question. Where is my treasure? What goals do I spend my day focusing on reaching? What do my actions show that my purpose is?

In the space below or on a separate sheet of paper, draw two houses with foundations.

On the first house foundation, write or draw what your foundation is in now. Remember, your foundation is anything where you find your identity, self-worth, or security. (For example, you may write in the foundation section things like career, people, financial status, what people think, etc.)

In the foundation of the second house, write in what you desire for your foundation to be in. When you're finished, think about this question:

If a storm were to come, which house foundation would stay secure?

Chapter 8 Reflection Questions

1. What do you feel like the biggest risk is in following God for you personally?

2. Where do you feel like our lack of trust in God at times comes from?

3. Can you think of a time when you felt "hurt" by something God allowed you to go through?

4. If you are able, write down the following phrase on a notecard and keep it somewhere you can see it consistently for an entire week. Each time within the week when you start to struggle with something or someone, grab the notecard and read it: *I am a child of God. And my worth, security, and hope is based on God being my Father...*

CHAPTER 9 ~ Worry & Fear

"I am leaving you with a gift- peace of mind and heart. And the peace I give is a gift the world cannot give. So don't be troubled or afraid."
~John 14:27(NLT)

Often we hear the same common phrases over and over again when we are struggling with worry. "Let Go and Let God." "God is in control." "Surrender it to God." And secretly, we may think, "If it were only that simple."

Worry is a huge struggle. There are very few people that don't struggle with worry in some way. Worry is defined as

"to feel uneasy or concerned about something; be troubled"

It seems that underlying most areas of worry there is some type of fear. For example, if a parent is worrying about their 16-year old daughter driving out of town for the first time, there is a fear that she may get hurt. If a student is worrying about a big test coming up, there is a fear that they may not score well on the test.

Think about your biggest worry right now, what is the *fear* underlying the worry? What are you afraid of? It seems that a lot of times our worries are connected to the same root fear.

What's amazing is how often prophets and people within Scripture struggle with fear. In fact, the phrase "do not be afraid" is used over 100 times in Scripture. Let's take a look at some examples.

The Battle of Worry

*"When you go out to fight your enemies and you face horses and chariots and an army greater than your own, **do not be afraid.** The Lord your God, who brought you out of the land of Egypt is with you! When you prepare for battle, the priest must come forward to speak to all the troops. He will say to them, 'Listen to me, all you men of Israel! **Do not be afraid** as you go out to fight your enemies today! **Do not lose heart or tremble** before them. For the Lord your God is going with you! He will fight for you against your enemies, and He will give you victory!'*
~Deuteronomy 20:1-4(NLT)

From what I've read, the majority of times God tells his people not to be afraid- it is followed by a promise. So here in this Scripture, God is revealing to the Israelites to not be afraid. Directly after this, he states "The Lord your God, who brought you out of the land of Egypt, is with you!" (vs.1) He follows his command to not be afraid, with a promise that he will be with them. They will not be alone in this battle.

Later, in verse three, he tells the Israelites again "Do not be afraid as you go out to fight your enemies today! Do not lose heart or panic or tremble before them." Here he brings up other forms of worry like panic and trembling. Panic is actually a form of anxiety. Again, he follows this with a promise.

"For the Lord your God is going with you! He will fight for you against your enemies, and He will give you victory!"
~Verse 4(NLT)

God must have known that the Israelites were trying to fight this battle on their own. He reminds them that he will fight the battle for them if only they would submit to him. How often do we do the same when it comes to our battles with worry? We try to fight the battle on our own through control, dwelling, overthinking, etc. An example of this is when we look to control the circumstances around us instead of submitting them to God. That can be a common way to deal with our fear instead of allowing God to help us with the fear.

However, everything we've discussed in this book up until this point fits into our struggle with submission to God. For example, if hurt from our past has transferred onto what we believe about God- why would we give him our worries? If we don't truly believe that he is good, why would we trust him? If the condition of our heart is filled with unfulfilled dreams, hurt, and doubt, why would we trust this God to fight the battle of worry for us?

If our foundation is not in our Father, why would we trust him with our worries?

We talked earlier about the common phrases used as advice for worry like "Let Go and Let God." The reason that it is not that simple is because our heart conditions need to be filled with trust first. Our foundation needs to be in the Father before we're able to let go and let God. That is why it is so important to allow God to heal our hearts and to experience more and more of his character.

I feel the need to add here a thought on anxiety/worry. You may have tendencies toward anxiety whether it's through genetics or something you've been through. If that is you, the concepts in this chapter may not "cure" your anxiety- you may always struggle with it in some way. However, these concepts could be tools and avenues to help cope.

Pray Instead of Worry

Don't worry about anything; instead, pray about everything.
Tell God what you need, and thank Him for all He has
done. Then you will experience God's peace, which exceeds
anything we can understand. His peace will guard
your hearts and minds as you live in Christ Jesus.
~Philippians 4:6-7(NLT)

I love this verse because it breaks down how to deal with worry into different steps. First, it says instead of worrying about things to pray about things. If we spent as much time praying about things as we did worrying about them, we would spend a lot of time communicating with our Father and a lot less time worrying.

The second sentence is very direct and says to "tell God what you need." So with the honesty of a child, simply tell God what your fear is. Tell him what you are afraid of with honesty. Be honest with yourself and then be honest with him. It can be easy to pray what you feel like the "correct" prayer is instead of just being real, as if talking to a best friend.

Next, we are to "thank Him for all He has done." Thank him for helping you. Thank him for listening to you share. Thank him for whatever it is you feel led to thank him for. Research has even shown that gratitude is beneficial to your health.

The remainder of this Scripture discusses God's peace. "Then you will experience God's peace which exceeds anything we can understand. His peace will guard your hearts and minds as you live in Christ Jesus."

When in your life do you remember sensing God's peace? How would you explain it? Would you describe it as exceeding anything you could understand?

When I meditate on the Scripture in "the child in the crowd" chapter, I often think of what the child would have been feeling when Jesus called him out of the crowd. There is one word that comes to mind.

Peace.

He will go ahead of you

*"So be strong and courageous! **Do not be afraid and do not panic before them.** For the Lord your God will personally go ahead of you. He will never fail you nor abandon you."*
~Deuteronomy 31:6(NLT)

Here the promise following the command to not be afraid is that God will personally go ahead of us. There is also a promise that he will never fail us or abandon us. Those are strong promises.

The story below is a visual picture of these promises. Pretend like you are the person that is lost in the story. If you are alone, it may help to read this story slowly and out loud:

I am lost in an unfamiliar land. I've tried every option to find my way home and it feels as if I am going in circles. I am so scared and am beginning to panic. What if I never see my family again? What if I never see my friends again? I am so afraid.

Wait! As I look forward, I see a man walking toward me. I've never seen him before but I feel like I've known him my whole life. I scream to him,

"Help! I don't know my way home!!"

He continues to walk toward me and the closer he gets, the more calm I feel. He has no sign of panic or fear. He looks me deeply in the eyes and asks me gently

"Can I help you find your way?"

I feel so calm, but my mind is reminding me that this man is a stranger and I don't know where he will lead me. So I thank him for the offer and continue on my way.

Night is beginning to hit and I am beginning to feel weak and hungry. The more time passes by, the more I begin to panic.

Up ahead, I see the same man from earlier walking toward me. He is so mysterious and my panic and fear calms in the same way it did earlier when I met him for the first time. He looks at me in the eyes again gently and asks

"Can I help you find your way?"

This time, I feel my heart softening toward this man even more, and out of my mouth comes the word

"Yes."

He smiles at me and says there is one thing that I must know. My eyes are filled with tears and I don't know why. He says:

"My name is Jesus. I will not tell you where I am taking you, but I promise it will be good and I will take care of your heart. Do you trust me?"

As he stares at me, I somehow feel that I have been searching for this man my whole life. As he looks at me, and I experience being in his presence, I can't help but trust him. So I respond:

"Yes, I trust you."

I take his hand and he leads me through this land. He didn't take me where I expected, but my heart is filled with peace because I am with him and he has become everything to me. The more I get to know this man and experience his love for me, the more I trust him and want to follow where he leads..

Chapter 9 Reflection Questions

1. In what ways do you personally try to battle worry on your own?

2. What is your biggest worry? What is the fear underlying the worry? What promise do you feel God showing you to help you with the fear?

3. When was a time in your life that sticks out as being a time when you experienced God's peace?

4. If there is a specific worry that you are really struggling with, try applying the steps outlined in Phillipians 4:6-7 (also described in the "Pray instead of Worry section in this chapter.) Below is an outline to help:

1. Pray instead of Worry:

2. Tell God What You Need:

3. Thank Him for all He has done:

4. Experience God's *peace*.

CHAPTER 10 ~A Jealous Father

"One day some parents brought their children to Jesus so He could touch and bless them. But the disciples scolded the parents for bothering Him. When Jesus saw what was happening, He was angry with His disciples. He said to them, "Let the children come to me. Don't stop them! For the Kingdom of God belongs to those who are like these children. I tell you the truth, anyone who doesn't receive the Kingdom of God like a child will never enter it. Then he took the children in His arms and placed His hands on their heads and blessed them."
~Mark 10: 13-16(NLT)

When I originally started this chapter, I had titled it "An Approachable Father." As I read through the verse above, I was struck at how approachable Jesus was. It's amazing how open Jesus is to the children approaching him, despite the disciples trying to step in.

But as I spent time in prayer and meditating on this verse, something new began to resonate in my spirit. God is not only approachable, but he is also a *jealous* God.

As I began to think about Scripture describing Jesus as getting *angry* with the disciples, I began to wonder what brought Jesus to such emotion. Jesus wasn't described as being frustrated, sad, or annoyed. He was described as being *angry*.

There is nothing more that Jesus wanted then for these children to simply be in his presence, experience him, and to be blessed. That concept is at the heart of everything Jesus teaches. There is nothing more that Jesus wants for *us* as his children than to be in his presence, experience him, and be blessed.

The word "jealous" in the Old and New Testament is also described as being zealous. So God is eager to protect what is precious to him. When the concept of God being a jealous God is used in Scripture it is often referring to being jealous of idols.

"You must not make for yourself an idol of any kind or an image of anything in the heavens or on the earth or in the sea. You must not bow down to them or worship them, for I, the Lord your God, am a jealous God who will not tolerate your affection for any other gods."
~Exodus 20:4-5(NLT)

Think of an idol as being something or someone that you worship more than God. The concept of this book is finding your identity in being a child of God. Is an identity similar to an idol? Is the Lord jealous of anything we put our identity in other than him?

When you are alone with Him

One way to check what your identity is in is to examine how you are when you are alone with God. Does the condition of your heart feel "settled?" Does it feel at peace? Regardless of what you struggle putting your identity in, your mind may wander to that identity.

Character is who you are when no other people are around. Is your character built on God or is your character built on a different identity? Do you find yourself thirsty for God when you are alone with him and in his presence? Or do you find yourself thirsty for the approval of man?

Another thing that seems to come to the surface when we are alone with God is the condition of our hearts and what we believe about God. (Discussed in earlier chapters) Does it *hurt* sometimes when you slow down to be with him? Like the pain you have been avoiding dealing with is all of a sudden so overwhelming?

God cherishes our time with him. If our heart and mind is filled with worshiping another besides him in that time, he is jealous. He wants us to be *completely his.*

The term jealousy when used by people often goes hand and hand with a sense of control. God's jealousy is not like human jealousy. It is healthy and not controlling. He knows that what is best for our heart is to be completely his. He wants what's best for us. But he won't force himself on us. He will wait. It's our choice whether we chose to be completely his or not.

Take a moment and think of that person, thing, or idea that kept coming to your mind throughout this book when you reflect on what you struggle putting your identity in besides God. Fill in that identity in the blank below without reading what is around it yet. Once it is filled in, picture God speaking this to you:

I am *jealous* of _____. Having your identity in it is keeping you from fully experiencing my love, presence, and blessings. It makes me *jealous* because I know the blessings and promises that I have for you. I know what will happen if you allow the foundation of your heart to fully be found in my love. Know if you let go of that identity, I will take care of you. I will be everything and more that you're searching for in that identity. I will fulfill every need and every desire. It may not be in the way you expect, but it will be *good*. I truly have your best interests at heart. Trust me, my child...

Let the Child Come

To close this chapter, let's take a look at another illustration. This may be what one of the children that was brought to Jesus in the verse beginning this chapter may have been feeling:

Today is the day! I have been counting down to this day where I can meet this man they call Jesus. I see him from a distance and we're getting closer and closer to him. I wonder what it will be like to stand next to him. What will I feel? What will I think? What will I say?

As we get closer, I see these men called disciples standing with him. They are staring at us with mean faces. I wonder why. We've finally reached Jesus, and now the disciples are telling my mom and dad to not bother Jesus with the other children and me. Why would they say that? I don't want to bug Jesus, I just want to be with him. I can feel my heart sink as I want so badly to be with him!

Wait! Jesus is yelling at them. He looks so mad. He told them to let my friends and I come to him and not to stop us! And that the disciples should receive the kingdom of heaven like us. The way he talked about us made me feel more protected then I've ever felt before.

Jesus walked over to me and picked me up and is holding me in his arms. I just want to stay in his arms forever and him to never let go. I've never felt anything like this before. He puts his hand on my head and I feel so warm inside. Sometimes when I'm feeling cold, I like to pull a blanket over me to keep me warm. As soon as Jesus touched my head, I felt that warm feeling.

I don't know much about this Jesus man but I do know I want to be just like him. I want to make people feel the way he is making me feel and teach people about him. I want to stay in his arms forever, I don't want him to let me down from his arms. As he lets me down, and we begin to walk away, he calls my name. I turn around and he gives me a gift and tells me not to look at it until I get home.

As I walk away, I begin to cry like I've never cried before. I feel so scared and I don't know why. I am going to miss Jesus so much. I want him to stay with me and never leave…

I walk into the house with tear-filled eyes, and open the gift that he gave me. It is a rock that fits in my hand. On one side it has a cross and on the other it says this:

I am leaving you with a gift-peace of mind and heart. And the peace I give is a gift the world cannot give. So don't be troubled or afraid. (Based on John 14:27(NLT))

Chapter 10 Reflection Questions

1. Have you ever had an experience where you knew God was "jealous" for you? If so, how did it make you feel?

2. As this book comes to close, do you feel like your heart is in a place of being completely his? If not, what is holding you back?

CONCLUSION

The Journey Continues

"Then He took the children in His arms and placed
His hands on their heads and blessed them."
~Mark 10:16(NLT)

I was considering naming this final conclusion-the journey comes to an end. Then, I realized that the journey is not coming to an end even though this book is ending. You and I will continue to learn about what it means to be a child of God and for God to be our Father throughout the rest of our lives. So the journey continues...

If you take a look at the Scripture above where Jesus is blessing the children- that is the promise I desire to leave you with. If you allow God to be your identity and are completely his, he will continually wrap you in his arms and bless you. The blessings may not always be in the way you expect, but he will bless you and take care of your heart.

What I've found in my journey of what it means to have your identity in God is something beautiful and simple. To be a child of God is to *be completely his.* And to allow God to be our Father is to *trust who he is.*

Who are you?

You are a child of God. That is who you are.

About the Author

Stacy Miller provides professional counseling in Columbus, Ohio. She specializes in working with children, teenagers, women, and families. Her passion is helping those who are hurting find restoration and emotional healing of their hearts. Stacy lives in Ohio with her husband and their dog, Sebastian.

References

Chapter 6

1. Gary Chapman, "The 5 Love Languages," April 18, 2011. http://www.5lovelanguages.com

Chapter 9

1. The Free Dictionary by Farlex, "Worry," April 18, 2011. http://www.thefreedictionary.com/worry

Made in United States
North Haven, CT
03 February 2026

87947725R00071